Bet You C
Do This!

Sandy Ransford lived in London and worked in publishing before becoming a full-time writer. She has written many books for children, including titles on puzzles and jokes, games and activities, conservation, animals and riding; as well as a number of stories. She now lives in rural mid-Wales with her architect husband, a horse, two ponies, two pygmy goats, two sheep and two cats.

Sally Kindberg is a writer and illustrator. Her children's books include *Tricky Tricks*, *Robotina Finds Out* and *Creepy Kokey*. She has worked for *The Independent*, *The Guardian* and the BBC. She loves travelling and writing about it – her trips have included sailing in a tall ships' race and going to Elfschool in Iceland. She collects robots, has a daughter called Emerald and is currently writing and illustrating a book of 'hairy tales'.

Other books by Macmillan

The Practical Joker's Handbook
John Dinneen

The Practical Joker's Handbook 2
John Dinneen

Pony Puzzles
Diana Kimpton

Puppy Puzzles
Sandy Ransford

Alien Puzzles
Sandy Ransford

Alien Jokes
Sandy Ransford

School Jokes
Sandy Ransford

Holiday Jokes
Sandy Ransford

Revolting Jokes
Sandy Ransford

Bet You Can't Do This!

Sandy Ransford

Illustrated by **Sally Kindberg**

MACMILLAN CHILDREN'S BOOKS

First published 2002
by Macmillan Children's Books
a division of Macmillan Publishers Limited
20 New Wharf Road, London N1 9RR
Basingstoke and Oxford
www.panmacmillan.com

Associated companies throughout the world

ISBN 0 330 39772 9

3 5 7 9 8 6 4

A CIP catalogue record for this book is available from the British Library.

Printed by Mackays of Chatham plc, Chatham, Kent.

Contents

Frankly Physical

Fool Your Friends

More Bamboozling

Absolutely Impossible

Heroic Hoaxes

Five-star Tricks

Introduction

Bet you can't do the tricks in this book! They all *sound* impossible – but wait. Spend a few minutes learning how to do them and you'll have a whale of a time impressing your friends.

Most of the tricks are very simple and require little or no equipment. Some are specially designed to fool friends and classmates; some require a bit of practice before you try them out on a gullible pal. A few – those in the Absolutely Impossible section – are genuinely impossible, but who knows, one or two of the geniuses among you might even manage to crack some of them. The Five-star Tricks at the end of the book *are* quite complicated, so only attempt them when you've played yourself in with the easier ones.

Bet you'll have lots of fun with this book, and that you *will* be able to do the tricks once you've read it!

uh?

Tricks with Props

Egg-o Trick

Can you make an egg stand on its end and spin like a top? I'll bet you can't!

You will need
Some eggs
A chopping-board
A saucepan
Some water
A cooker

1. Take an egg from the fridge. Put it on a chopping-board, hold its rounded end downwards and try to spin it round. Can you?

2. I thought not! But there is a way to do it.

3. Hard-boil an egg (i.e. cook it in boiling water for about 10 minutes), then let it cool and try the trick again.

4. Hey presto, it works!

It's a good trick to try on a friend, as you can hide your hard-boiled egg among some uncooked ones. Make sure your friend chooses one of the raw eggs, while you demonstrate your prowess with the hard-boiled one. They will be amazed!

The Diving Cork

A cork floats on the surface of water, we all know that. Now, can you sink a cork in a bowl of water without touching it, either with your hands or with anything else?

You will need
A bowl of water
A cork
A drinking glass

1. Half fill the bowl with water and put the cork on the surface, where it will float.

2. Turn the glass upside down and lower it slowly over the cork.

3. As you do this the cork will move downwards. It will still be on the water's surface, but the level of the surface under the glass will be lower than that in the bowl. The cork will appear to be floating underwater.

Walking Water

Can you make water 'walk' along a piece of string? (NB In case you don't succeed first time, practise this trick over the sink.)

You will need
A jug
A glass
A piece of string about 1 metre long
Some water

1. Fill the jug about two-thirds full of water. Wet the string and tie one end of it to the handle of the jug.

2. Put the glass on a draining board in front of you, about 60cm from the jug.

3. Now pull the string across the spout of the jug and place the other end in the glass. Hold it against the side of the glass so it is kept taut.

4. Lift the jug about 30cm up in the air and gently pour the water along the string. Provided you keep the string taut by holding it in the glass the water will travel along the string to the glass without spilling.

Bending Water

I'll bet you can't make a stream of water bend the way you want it to.

You will need
A plastic pen
A woolly jumper
A tap

1. Turn on the tap until you have a very thin stream of water.

2. Wrap the woolly jumper round the pen and rub it vigorously up and down for a few moments.

3. Hold the pen near the top of the stream of water coming out of the tap, but do not put it into the stream of water.

4. Move the pen around – and you will find that the stream of water bends in the direction of your pen, and you can make it go in any direction you like. It is the static electricity produced by rubbing the pen on the jumper that attracts the stream of water towards it.

Climbing Through Paper

Can you climb through an A4-sized sheet of paper? You can if you know how!

You will need
An A4-sized sheet of paper
A pair of scissors

1. It sounds impossible, but you don't need to be

tiny to do this. First, fold the paper in half lengthways.

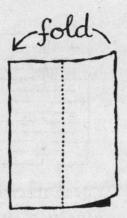

2. Next, cut the paper from alternate sides not quite all the way across, as shown in the diagram.

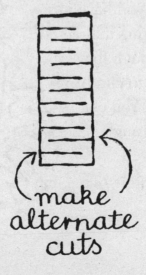

3. Open out the paper and cut along the fold, leaving the edges uncut.

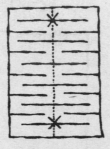

cut along
folds between
crosses

4. Carefully open out the paper, and you will discover you have made a ring that is large enough for an adult to climb through. You can climb through an A4-sized sheet of paper!

fun!

Impossible Loop

If I bet you you can't divide a loop of paper into two separate loops by cutting it you will think it a very easy bet to win. But try it and see – it will surprise you.

You will need
A sheet of paper
Adhesive tape
A pair of scissors

1. Cut a strip of paper about 30cm long and 3cm wide.
2. Make one twist in the paper and stick the two ends together with a piece of adhesive tape to make a loop.
3. Now cut along the centre of the loop, as if you were trying to divide the strip into two separate loops.
4. No matter how many times you try it you will be left with a single large loop of paper!

By twisting the paper you have made a Mobius strip, named after the 19th-century German scientist who discovered it. The shape has intrigued scientists for many years.

Water into Lemonade

Can you turn water into lemonade? I can!

You will need
A large pottery or enamel jug (not glass)
Two small sponges
Some absorbent kitchen cloths
A plastic drinking mug
A drinking glass
Some water
Some lemonade
A piece of Blu-tack

1. Prepare the jug beforehand. Stick the Blu-tack on the base of the plastic mug, fill it with lemonade and stand it inside the jug. Press the Blu-tack down firmly. Pack the sponges and the absorbent cloths round the mug so they hold it firmly in place.

2. Fill a glass with water and show it to your friends. Tell them you can turn it into lemonade by pouring it into the jug. They, of course, will not believe you.

3. Pour the water carefully into the jug so it misses the plastic mug and goes on to the sponges and cloths. They will absorb the water. Practise this first so you can see how much water they will soak up and add more cloths or sponges if necessary.

press firmly

4. Then say to your friends, 'I'll just wave my hand over the jug, and the water will turn into lemonade.'

5. Then tip up the jug and pour it into the glass – and, sure enough, it is lemonade! Because, of course, you are really pouring the lemonade out of the mug inside the jug.

Getting the Point

Can you put the tips of two pencils together? Of course you can! Ah, but try doing it with one eye closed. I'll bet you can't!

You will need
Two sharp pencils

1. Hold the pencils in front of you, with the points facing each other, about 60cm apart.

2. Bring the pencils slowly together so their points touch. Can you do it?

3. If you can, try again keeping one eye closed. This is much more difficult and it is doubtful if you will succeed. Because each of your eyes focuses on a slightly different point, you need both of them to judge distance accurately.

Seeing Double

This trick can make you see double – and perhaps even treble!

You will need

A sheet of paper

A pin

1. Using the pin, make two small holes about 1.5mm apart in the corner of the paper.

2. Stand in a good light and hold the paper close up to one eye. In your other hand hold the pin behind and close to the paper.

3. Look through the holes at the pin. Move it back from the paper until it is about 6cm away – what you thought was one pin has suddenly become two!

4. If you make a third hole in the paper above or below the original two so they form a triangle shape, you may be able to see three pins when you look through the holes. Try moving the pin a few centimetres away from the paper.

Matchless Strength

I bet you can't break a matchstick in two with your fingers. Not the way described here, anyway.

You will need
A matchstick

1. Place the matchstick across the back of your middle finger and underneath your first and third fingers so it rests on the joints nearest to your fingertips.

2. Now push upwards with your middle finger and downwards with the other two fingers and see if you can break the matchstick. I'll bet you can't!

3. The only way you will manage to break the matchstick is to move it closer to your knuckles, because then your fingers will have the power they need. It's all a matter of leverage.

Playing Card with Four Sides

A playing card has just two sides, doesn't it? Well, believe it or not, you can make one that appears to have four sides.

You will need
Some plain white card
A pair of scissors
A pencil
A ruler
Some paint or a marker pen

1. Make the playing card by ruling the shape on to the sheet of white card and then cutting it out. Paint or draw the symbols on it as shown in the diagram. You can draw diamonds or hearts (red), or clubs or spades, as shown here, (black).

2. The fun with this is showing it to a friend. You show side 1, which is apparently an ace.

3. Then show side 2, which is apparently a six.

4. Then show side 3, which is apparently a three.

5. And lastly show side 4, which appears to be a four.

6. You need to practise these steps because the success of the trick lies in the way you hold the card.

Which Way?

Here's a really amazing challenge. Draw a galloping horse on a piece of paper and then, without touching it, make the horse go in the opposite direction.

You will need
A sheet of paper
A pen or pencil
A straight-sided glass
A jug of water

1. Fold the paper in half and draw the galloping horse in the centre of one side of it. (If you can't draw a horse, don't worry, draw something else.)

2. Stand the drawing on the table like a greetings card. Place the glass about 10cm in front of it. Now make the horse go in the opposite direction without touching the paper or the glass.

3. Here's how to do it. Fill the glass with water from the jug, and look at the drawing through the glass.

4. You will discover that the horse is now galloping in the opposite direction!

Mad Maths

Lay out 18 matchsticks in the pattern shown in the diagram below. Can you take away nine and leave ten on the table?

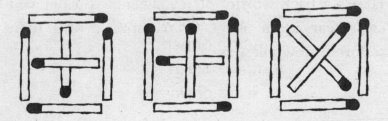

You will need

18 matchsticks

1. Lay out the 18 matchsticks as shown. Now, nine from 18 doesn't equal ten, does it? Yet there is a simple way to do this.

2. You move the matchsticks shown as dotted lines in the diagram below – leaving TEN! Could you do it?

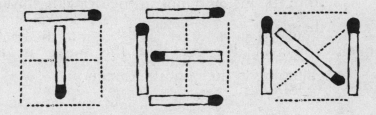

Magic Paper

Here's a trick worthy of a magician. I'll bet you can't tear up a sheet of newspaper and then restore it to wholeness.

You will need

Two copies of the same newspaper
Paper glue

1. The challenge is to tear a sheet of newspaper into little pieces, say, 'Abracadabra,' and then open it up again in one piece.

2. This is how to do it. Take the front and back pages off both your newspapers. Fold up one sheet as small as you can, holding it face upwards as you start, and glue it to the back of the second sheet of newspaper as shown in the diagram.

3. Keeping the folded sheet at the back of the paper, tear up the second sheet, putting the pieces in front of the folded sheet as you do so.

4. When you have torn up the paper, crumple the pieces into a ball and manoeuvre them so the folded sheet is uppermost in your hand.

5. Unfold the folded sheet, keeping the torn pieces hidden in your hand. Your torn-up sheet is now whole again!

Frankly
Physical

Flying Arms

If you do the trick described below I bet you can't keep your arms down by your sides in a relaxed position afterwards. Try it and see.

You will need
A doorway

1. Stand in the open doorway with your arms down by your sides. Then press the backs of your hands hard against the doorposts, keeping your arms straight.
2. Stand in this position, keeping the backs of your hands pressed against the doorposts, while you count slowly up to 30. Or time yourself with a watch for half a minute.
3. Relax your arms and step out of the doorway. Now, without tensing up your arms, see if you can keep them by your sides. You will find it is almost impossible, as they want to fly up into the air!

flap

flap

Hands Up!

You can play a variation of the above trick on a friend, betting them that you can make them obey your commands. If you can hide a toy water pistol in your pocket, so much the better!

You will need
A friend
A toy water pistol

1. Hide the water pistol in your pocket, and bet your friend you can make him or her do whatever you want.

2. Ask them to stretch both their arms out in front of them, with the palms of their hands facing each other. Stand opposite them and cup your hands round theirs.

3. Ask your friend to push the backs of their hands against yours, keeping their arms stretched out straight in front of them, while you count up to 50.

4. When you have done so, move your hands, brandish your water pistol, and say, 'Hands up!' They will be amazed that their hands automatically obey your command!

Can You Make Your Arms Shrink?

Well, can you? I can!

You will need
A wall

1. Stand facing a wall, holding out your arms in front of you so that your fingertips just touch the wall.

2. Keeping your arms straight, slowly swing them down, back behind you, pushing them back quite hard, then forward again. Do this a couple of times, without moving your feet.

3. Still keeping your feet still, swing your arms forward to touch the wall again.

Do they still reach it? The chances are that your arms will apparently have shrunk!

Samson's Finger

Samson was amazingly strong, and with this trick you can prove that your little finger is as strong as his must have been!

You will need
A friend
A chair

1. Ask your friend to sit down in the chair with their head back and their chin up.

2. Place your little finger on your friend's forehead, and ask him or her to try to stand up without moving sideways or wriggling.

3. Provided your friend doesn't cheat, he or she will be unable to move from the chair. Your little finger should be quite strong enough to keep them in the chair.

Although this seems amazing, it is because, in order to stand up, your friend would first have to move their head slightly forwards, and your little finger is quite strong enough to prevent this movement.

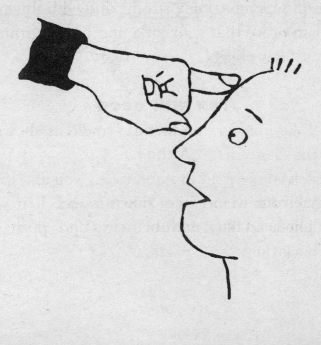

Strong-arm Tactics

If you have a friend who is bigger and stronger than you are, challenge them to beat you at this trick.

You will need
A friend
A broom handle

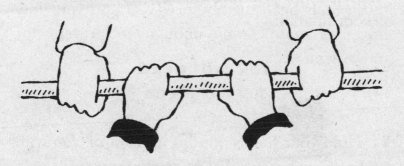

1. Take hold of the broom handle as shown in the diagram.
2. Ask your friend to stand facing you and to put their hands on either side of yours.
3. Then challenge your friend to push you backwards.

4. If they are stronger than you it would seem to be no contest – but not if you know what to do. Instead of pushing back against your friend, lift the broom handle upwards. They should then find it impossible to meet the challenge.

Scissors

This trick with your fingers really tests your powers of coordination.

You will need
Just your fingers

1. Hold your hands out flat in front of you with your fingers together facing downwards.
2. Starting with whichever hand you find easier (e.g. if you are right-handed, your right hand) try moving your index (first) finger away from the others, then bring it back again.
3. Then try moving your little finger away from the others and back again.

4. Now move your first and second fingers, and third and fourth fingers apart, so your hand resembles a pair of scissors, and bring them back again.

5. Now keep your middle two fingers together, and move your index finger and little finger away and back again at the same time.

6. All right so far? Right, now have a go with the other hand. Once you can do these movements, concentrate on doing movements 4 and 5 in sequence with both hands.

7. And if you can do that, I'll bet you can't do this! With your right hand, carry out movement 4, and with your left hand movement 5, *at the same time.*

What Big Feet You've Got!

Here's a trick to play on someone who has big feet – perhaps your father or elder brother.

You will need
A big-footed person

A wall
A chair

1. Ask your big-footed friend to stand facing the wall and then to back four foot-lengths away from it.

2. Put the chair against the wall in front of them and ask them to lean over until their forehead rests against the wall above the chair.

3. Then ask them to pick up the chair and return to a standing position without moving their feet and without touching the wall with anything but their head.

4. If they have big enough feet, they will find the task impossible. On the other hand, if you have small feet, you will manage it quite easily. Your poor big-footed friend will be baffled!

find someone with big feet

Don't try this trick on anyone who has a bad back – it could make it worse.

Eye, Eye!

Here's a simple little trick you can try yourself, and then see if a friend can do it.

You will need
Just your eyes

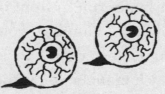

1. Close your eyes.
2. Now roll your eyeballs up as far as you can, as if you were trying to see something on top of your head.
3. Keeping your eyeballs in that position, try to open your eyes.
4. You can't, can you? (Or if you can, you cheated!) It's all to do with your eye muscles,

and it isn't possible to open your eyes with your eyeballs in that position.

Finger Maths

Do you have trouble multiplying by nine? Here's an easy way to do it.

You will need
Two hands

1. Hold your hands out in front of you with the palms upwards. Number your fingers and thumbs from left to right 1 to 10.
2. Decide which number you want to multiply by nine, and bend down the finger bearing that number.
3. Count the fingers on either side of the finger you have bent down. They will give you the answer to your sum. For example, if you want to multiply nine by two, bend down your left index finger (i.e. finger number 2). The fingers on either side of it number one and eight – 18 – which is the answer to the sum of nine

multiplied by two. If you want to multiply nine by three, bend down the middle finger of your left hand, and you will have two fingers on the left of it and seven on the right – 27.

All Fall Down?

Do you think you are strong enough to resist the combined pressure of ten people? Try this, you might be.

You will need
Ten friends
A wall

1. Stand facing a wall and put your hands out in front of you to rest them, palms flat, against the wall.
2. Invite your friends to stand behind you, one behind the other, each with their hands on the shoulders of the person in front of them.
3. Now tell them all to push. You might imagine that you'll be squashed against the wall, but you won't. In fact, you'll easily withstand the

combined pressure of all your friends. It sounds unlikely, but each person absorbs the pressure of the person behind them, and no one will be pushed over.

Testing the Water

You can tell the difference between hot and cold, can't you? I bet you can't if you try this test!

You will need
3 plastic bowls
Hot and cold water

1. Half fill the bowls with water. One should contain hot (but not so hot you can't put your hand in it) water, one cold water, and one lukewarm water.

2. Put one hand in the bowl of hot water and the other in the bowl of cold. Keep your hands in the water for a few minutes.

put hand in

3. Then remove both hands from their bowls and put them both in the bowl of lukewarm water. Does it feel lukewarm?

4. In fact, the hand that was previously in the hot water will tell you the lukewarm water is cold; and the hand that was previously in the cold water will tell you that the lukewarm water is hot. Can you still tell hot from cold?

Fingertip Strength

Challenge a friend to test the strength of your fingertips, secure in the knowledge that you will win.

You will need
A friend

1. Standing with your feet apart, put your arms in front of you so that the tips of your index (first) fingers touch (see the diagram overleaf).

2. Get your friend to grasp each of your wrists in one of his or her hands, and then challenge him or her to pull your fingertips apart. No matter how hard they try, they won't be able to do so!

Long Tongue

Bet a friend they cannot stick out their tongue and touch their nose.

You will need
A friend

1. Make your bet as described above. Your friend

will stick out their tongue until it aches, trying desperately to reach the tip of their nose. They may even push down the tip of their nose to try and make it reach their tongue!

2. When they give up and say it's not possible, you reply, 'Oh yes it is. I can do it.'

And to prove it, you stick out your tongue and touch your nose – with a finger!

Hand Clasp

Bet your friend that you can make them clasp their hands together in such a way that they won't be able to get out of the room without unclasping them.

You will need
A friend
A heavy piece of furniture

1. Make the bet in a room where there is a heavy piece of furniture, such as a large table or a sideboard.

2. Take your friend over to the furniture and clasp their hands round one of its legs. They then won't be able to leave the room without unclasping them!

Fool Your
Friends

Tiny Person

Here's a challenge that sounds impossible. Bet your friend that he or she cannot push themselves through a keyhole!

You will need
A piece of paper
A pencil
A friend

1. Your friend will agree that pushing themselves through a keyhole is impossible. However, you say that of course you can push yourself through a keyhole.

2. Write your name on a scrap of paper, fold it, and push it through the keyhole. Hey Presto! You have pushed yourself through a keyhole!

Tantalizing

Here's another tease to try on a friend. Find out their favourite chocolate bar before you try it.

You will need

A friend

A wall

A chocolate bar (or a 50p piece)

1. Ask your friend to stand with their back against a wall, with their feet together and the backs of their heels just touching the wall.
2. Place the chocolate bar or money about 30cm in front of their feet.
3. Now say, 'I bet you can't pick up that chocolate/money without moving your feet or bending your knees.'
4. They will try – but they will fail. It simply isn't possible to do without falling over.

Elbow Power

Can you write with your elbow, or with your toes? Or, for that matter, with your nose? I can!

You will need

A piece of paper

A pencil
A friend

1. Challenge a friend to write with their elbow (or toes, or nose). Tell them you can do it, and make a play of putting your elbow (or toes, or nose) on a piece of paper and making scribbling movements with it.

2. Meanwhile, have ready a piece of paper on which you have written 'With my elbow (or toes, or nose)'.

3. When your friend can stand the suspense no longer, produce the piece of paper.

Don't try this on the same friend you bamboozled with the pushing yourself through the keyhole trick.

famous author?

Through the Hole

This challenge seems impossible – until you know how to do it!

You will need
A friend
A piece of paper
A pair of scissors

1. Cut a small hole, measuring no more than 5mm across, in the centre of a piece of paper. Say to a friend, 'I bet you can't push a finger through the centre of this paper without tearing it.'
2. Your friend will look at the hole, examine their finger, and assume the challenge is impossible. 'I can do it,' you boast.
3. Roll the paper into a tube, and push your finger into its centre. You have pushed your finger through the centre of the paper without tearing it!

Never Seen Before or Since

Astound your friends with an amazing discovery!

You will need
A nut in its shell
A pair of nutcrackers
A friend

1. Say to a friend, 'I'm going to show you something that has never before been seen by anyone, and soon will never be seen by anyone again.'

2. Your friend will wonder what on earth you are going to do. But it's very simple. Take the nut out of your pocket and crack it with the nutcrackers (if you have a peanut you won't need nutcrackers).

3. Hold the nut up in the air. Say, 'This has never been seen before.'

4. Then pop the nut in your mouth and eat it. And say, 'And now it will never be seen again!'

Changing Colour

Can you change a green balloon into a white balloon?

You will need
Some green balloons
Some white balloons
A pin
A pencil
Friends

1. Slide a white balloon on to the pencil, then slide a green balloon over the top of it. Take away the pencil. Repeat with the other balloons.
2. Blow up the white balloons first and tie them up. If you are not very good at blowing up balloons, ask an adult to help. You can even buy a little pump to do it with.
3. Then blow up the green balloons a bit larger than the white ones. (They will have stretched anyway as you blew up the white ones.)
4. Show them to your friends as green balloons,

then challenge them to make them change colour.

5. Holding the pin concealed in your hand, prick each green balloon – and it will change into a white one!

Stuck to the Ceiling

And can you make balloons apparently stick to the ceiling?

You will need
Some balloons
A woolly jumper

1. Blow up the balloons and tie up the ends.
2. Rub them on the jumper.
3. Hold them near to the ceiling or near to a wall and they will stay there as if glued in place.

This is due to the static electricity caused when you rubbed them against the jumper.

Long Jump

There are lots of different ways of carrying out this challenge to your friend.

You will need
A friend
A road or river

1. If you are standing near a river with a bridge, or a road with a crossing, you can try this trick on a friend. Bet them they cannot jump across the river or road.
2. Unless the river is a tiny stream, your friend will know the challenge is impossible. But, of course, you tell them you can do it.
3. All you need to do is to cross the river or road by the bridge or crossing, and then do a little jump up into the air. You have jumped across the river!

Higher and Higher

If you managed to fool your friend with the previous trick, try this one on them.

You will need
A friend

1. Say to your friend, 'I bet you I can jump higher than a telegraph pole.'
2. Your friend, thinking this is impossible, will bet you that you can't.
3. But you can be certain of winning. As you will tell your friend, anyone can jump higher than a telegraph pole, as a telegraph pole can't jump!

Aristotle's Trick

If you cross your fingers and touch a marble with them, you'll feel as though you're touching two marbles!

You will need
A marble

1. Cross your first and second fingers. Put the marble on the table, and touch it with your fingertips. It will feel as if you are touching two marbles! It sometimes helps if you close your eyes so you cannot see there is really only one marble.

This odd little trick was first discovered by the Greek philosopher Aristotle over 2,000 years ago.

Thumbs Up

Bet a friend he or she cannot do this trick. I'll bet you can't either!

You will need
A friend

1. Tell your friend to put their right thumb across the palm of their right hand, making sure it is touching their palm.
2. Keeping their thumb in this position, tell your friend to put their hand up so their fingertips touch the underneath of their right armpit.
3. Tell him or her to move their thumb away from the palm of their hand, while still keeping their hand up under their arm.
4. Then tell him or her to put their thumb back into the exact position it was in across the palm of their hand. I'll bet they can't do it!

Knot Easy

Here's a challenge that seems impossible, but is simple when you know how to do it.

You will need
A friend
A length of string

1. The challenge is this: can you tie a knot in a piece of string without letting go of either end? You might like to try it yourself before betting a friend they can't do it.
2. After a few minutes of getting in a terrible muddle, here's how to do it. Put the string within easy reach, then fold your arms across your chest.
3. Take hold of the left-hand end of the string with your right hand and the right-hand end of the string with your left hand.
4. Keeping hold of the string, unfold your arms.
5. What's happened? There is a knot in the string!

Dicey Problem

This trick is very impressive, but really very simple to do.

You will need
Two dice
A friend

1. If you stand one die on top of the other, can you say what the total of the numbers on the three hidden sides are? It's easy when you know how.

2. If you try this challenge on a friend, they may think you have special dice, or have arranged them in a special way, but you can answer the question using any dice. The secret is that the spots on any two opposite sides of a die add up to seven. This means that if you can see a four, there is a three on the opposite face; if you can see a five, there is a two, and so on.

3. Therefore, to find out the total of the spots on the hidden sides, look at the number on the top surface of the upper die and subtract it from 14 (i.e. twice seven). The answer you get

will be the total of the spots on the three hidden sides of the dice. It looks like magic, but it just requires a little simple maths.

Hidden Coin

Bet a friend that you can put a coin somewhere that everyone in the room will be able to see except him or her.

You will need
A group of friends
A coin
A room without a mirror

1. Have you guessed where you should put the coin? On top of your friend's head! But keep them guessing for a while before you tell them!

Hidden Hand

Bet another friend that they cannot put their left hand somewhere their right hand cannot reach it.

You will need
A friend

1. Again, don't let your friend know how to do this too quickly – you can have a lot of fun watching their contortions as they stretch all over the place trying to solve the problem.
2. Have you guessed the answer? It is to put their left hand *on their right elbow*. If your friend does this, and keeps it in place, there is no way that their right hand can reach it.

More Bamboozling

Number Challenge

This trick tests someone's mathematical abilities.

1. Give your friend the pencil and paper, and say to them, 'You've got ten seconds to do this. Write down 13 thousand, 13 hundred and 13.'

2. Now, unless your friend is very clued-up, mathematically speaking, the chances are they will not be able to do this. Because, of course, 13 thousand, 13 hundred and 13 is in fact 14,313.

$$
\begin{array}{r}
13,000 \\
1,300 \\
13 \\
\hline
14,313
\end{array}
$$

Singing Underwater

Bet a friend they can't sing underwater. Can you do it?

You will need
A glass of water
A friend

1. Your friend doesn't need to be able to dive, or even to swim. Though a visit to the swimming pool is a good time to make the challenge! If they are able to dive they may even try to sing underwater, though you'd better warn them they will choke if they try to do so. But there are much simpler ways.

2. One is to hold the glass of water over your head and sing while holding it. You are singing under water!

3. The second is just to open your mouth and sing out loud, 'Underwater!'

Don't Spill It!

Can you knock a cup of tea on the floor without spilling it?

You will need
A cup of tea or glass of water
A friend

1. If you challenge a friend to do this, take them out into the garden just in case they make a mess. Don't, whatever you do, try it on a carpeted floor, in case you upset your mum!

2. The secret, of course, is just to put the cup of tea or glass of water on the ground, kneel down beside it, pick it up and knock it gently on the ground two or three times. You have knocked it on the ground without spilling it!

Look, No Hands

This trick might make your friends rather cross!

You will need
A table
A glass of lemonade
A box, hat or tea cosy
Friends

1. Stand the glass of lemonade on the table and cover it with the box, hat or tea cosy. It doesn't matter what you use as long as it hides the glass.
2. Then bet your friends you can drink the lemonade without touching the box or hat or tea cosy.
3. Of course, they won't believe you. So climb under the table, put your mouth up towards the glass above, and make slurping noises, as if you were drinking the lemonade.

4. After a few moments, come out from under the table. Wipe your mouth and say, 'Ah, that's better! I was really thirsty!'

5. One of your friends is bound, at this stage, to lift up the box, hat or tea cosy to see if you really have drunk the lemonade. When they do, grab the glass and drink it! You will then have drunk it without touching the hat, box or tea cosy, just as you bet them you could!

What Did You Say?

Can you predict what someone is going to say next? Bet a friend that you can!

You will need
A piece of paper
A pencil
A friend

1. Go up to a friend and say, 'I bet I can tell you exactly what you are going to say next.'

2. The chances are your friend will reply, 'What?'

3. And as they do so, produce a piece of paper from behind your back on which you have written in large letters, 'WHAT'.

4. You have done exactly as you said you would, and predicted what they would say next!

All Tied Up

Challenge a friend to get free from the position shown in the diagram overleaf.

You will need
A friend
Two lengths of string, each about 1 metre long

1. Tie each end of one of the pieces of string to your friend's wrists.

2. Loop the second piece of string round the first piece and ask your friend to tie the ends to your own wrists.

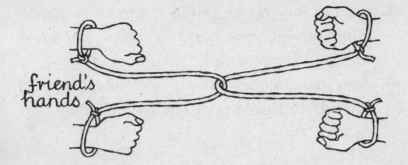

friend's
hands

3. Now challenge your friend to get free without untying the string. He or she will try all kinds of contortions.

4. This is how you do it. With your right hand get hold of the string that connects your friend's wrists. Push it through the loop on the inside of your own left wrist and towards the palm of your left hand.

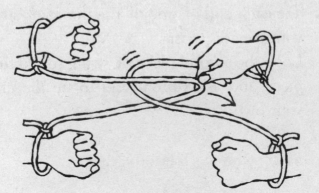

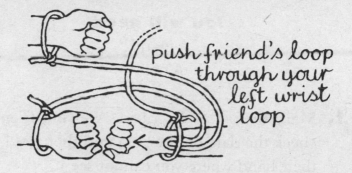

push friend's loop through your left wrist loop

5. Pass the string over the fingers of your left hand – and you are free!

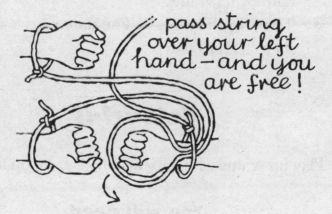

pass string over your left hand – and you are free!

Blind Date

Bet a friend that if they take a coin out of their pocket you can tell them the date.

You will need
A friend
A coin

1. Make the bet as described. Ask your friend to check the date on the coin and then hold it in their hand where you cannot see it.
2. Make a great show of closing your eyes and concentrating really hard, as if you can tell the date by telepathy.
3. Then say, 'I've got it! The date is . . . ' and tell them today's date!

Colourful

Play this game with a friend who is keen on football.

You will need
A friend

1. Bet your friend that you can make them say the word 'blue'.
2. They will take on the bet, thinking it a simple task to win.

3. Say to them, 'What are the colours of Manchester United?'
4. Your friend will reply, 'Red and white.'
5. Whereupon you retort, 'I told you I could make you say the word "red", didn't I?'
6. 'No you didn't,' your friend will reply. 'You bet me you could make me say the word "blue".'
7. 'And I just did!' you reply cheerfully.

Looking Up

Bet your friend that you can make everyone look in the same direction. You can play this trick at school or out in the street.

You will need
People to play the trick on

1. All you need do is look up at the sky. Touch a friend on the arm and point upwards. It's a fair bet that anyone passing will also look upwards.
2. As other people see you, your friend and the

passers-by looking up, they will follow suit. Soon everyone will be looking up at the sky! It's an old trick but it never fails to work.

Eleven Fingers

Tell your friend you have eleven fingers.

You will need
A friend

1. In front of your friend, count from one to ten on your fingers.
2. Then count backwards on one hand, 'Ten, nine, eight, seven, six . . . and five on the other hand makes eleven!' You have proved you have eleven fingers!

Easy Money

If your friend has very quick reflexes they may win this bet and make some money out of you, but it is very unlikely that they will do so.

You will need
A friend
A £5 note or a piece of paper the same size

1. Hold the note or equivalent sized piece of paper by its end.

2. Ask your friend to put a thumb and first finger on either side of the lower end of the note without touching it. Tell them you are going to drop the note, and that if their reflexes are fast enough and they can catch it between their thumb and forefinger they can keep it.

3. Start talking to your friend. It doesn't matter much what you say, but while you are saying it, without any warning, suddenly let go of the note.

4. It is very unlikely that you will lose your bet and therefore your note, but if you are worried, try it out with a piece of paper a few times first.

Mathematical Mind-reading I

Tell your friend that you can read their mind while they carry out complicated calculations in their head, and, no matter what they do, you will be able to say the answer.

You will need
A friend

1. Ask your friend to think of a number. Any number will do.
2. Now tell them to double it.
3. Ask them to multiply the result by three.
4. Ask them to add 200.
5. Ask them to take away the number they first thought of.
6. Then say that your powers are so great that you will be able to say the answer, and do just that. Say, 'The answer!'

Mathematical Mind-reading II

Again, persuade your friend that if they carry out your instructions you will be able to read their mind.

You will need
Two sheets of paper
Two pens or pencils

1. Give your friend one of the sheets of paper and a pen or pencil and ask them to write down a three-digit number. The only proviso is that the digits must decrease in number, such as 871.

2. Then ask them to write the same number backwards underneath the first number, e.g. 178.

3. Ask your friend to subtract the second number from the first and write down the answer, in our case, 693.

4. Ask them what the last digit is, i.e. 3.

5. You will then be able to tell them that the complete answer is 693. You do this by knowing the final digit, which you write down on your paper and subtract from 9 to find the first digit, in our case, 9 – 3 = 6. The middle digit is always 9.

← knows the answer

Absolutely
Impossible

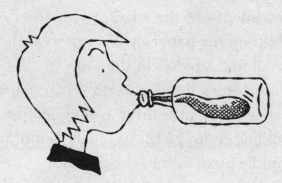

Tearing Off a Strip

This trick proves how strong a sheet of paper is – or how weak you are!

You will need
A sheet of paper
A pair of scissors

1. Fold the paper equally into three, then cut along each fold to within a couple of centimetres of the edge.

2. Hold up the paper by its corners with the two small uncut pieces at the top.

3. Now comes the challenge – can you pull the paper apart into three pieces so you are left holding one piece in each hand and the middle piece falls to the ground?

4. The answer is almost certainly 'no'. What happens is that one side will tear before the other, so you will be left with one third in one hand and two thirds in the other. To perform the trick you would have to make each cut exactly the same length, and pull with exactly the same amount of force with each hand. This is practically impossible to do.

Fold It Away

How many times can you fold a piece of paper?

You will need
A piece of paper

1. The challenge is to fold a piece of paper in half more than six times. It sounds easy, doesn't it? Surely anyone could do it? Try it and see.
2. You will start off easily, but after the fourth fold it gets more difficult. By the sixth, it is virtually impossible to continue. And it doesn't make any difference how thick or thin the paper is. By the time you have got to the sixth fold you are dealing with 64 thicknesses of paper – and that is very difficult to fold again.

Beaten by a Balloon

You can blow up a balloon, can't you? Try doing it this way and see what your answer is.

You will need
A balloon
A bottle

1. Blow a little air into the balloon and stretch it to make it easy to handle.
2. Put the balloon inside the bottle, folding the top of the balloon over the neck of the bottle.
3. Here's the challenge – with the balloon inside the bottle, can you blow it up?

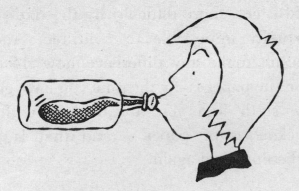

The answer will almost certainly be 'no', because the pressure of the air trapped inside the bottle is greater than the pressure you put on the balloon as you blow into it.

Wall Power

Do you think that standing by a wall could stop you moving your feet? Try this trick and see.

You will need
A wall

1. Stand with your left side against a wall. Move close enough to the wall for both your left foot and the left-hand side of your face to touch it.
2. In this position, try to lift your right foot off the ground.

Surprisingly, you will find you cannot do it. This is because in order to lift up your right foot, you first need to move your body slightly to the left, and, of course, you cannot do this because the wall is in the way.

Flying Paper

You'd imagine you can blow a piece of paper in any direction you want, wouldn't you?

You will need
A strip of paper measuring about 30cm x 4cm

1. Hold the 4cm end of the strip of paper up to your lips and blow on it, trying to blow it downwards towards the floor.

2. What happens? The paper flies upwards. You will find that however hard you blow, and whether you blow over the top of the paper or below it, it will still go up rather than down.

This phenomenon applies to aircraft wings as well as strips of paper, and is used by engineers when working out their designs.

Quite a Handful!

It's easy to crumple up a ball of paper with one hand, isn't it?

You will need
A double page of a broadsheet newspaper
(e.g. *The Times* or *The Guardian*)

1. Put the sheet of newspaper on a table and, using one hand only, try to crumple it up into a ball. You are not allowed to use your other hand, or clutch it against your chest, your knees or the table.

2. The chances are you will find it impossible. Try it and see. If you have very small hands, try the trick with a double page of a tabloid newspaper (e.g. The *Daily Mail* or *The Sun*).

Getting the Lemon

Can you whistle? Of course you can! Try this little trick and see if you can still whistle.

You will need
A lemon
A knife

1. Slice the lemon in half with the knife and suck hard on one half of it, letting the juice run round your mouth.
2. Now try to whistle. The chances are that your lips simply won't go into the right shape for whistling no matter how hard you try.

You can play a sneaky trick on a friend who whistles by sucking on a lemon in front of them. Because they will imagine the taste in their own mouths, they, too, will be unable to whistle.

Absolutely Crackers!

This trick is especially for biscuit lovers. You can eat three cream crackers in a minute, can't you? If you were very hungry you could probably eat them in half a minute. Or could you?

You will need
Three cream crackers
A watch

1. Note the time with a watch. Then start on your first cracker. When you've finished it, start on the second.

2. Check the watch. Can you eat the third before the minute is up? You're not allowed to have a drink of water until you've finished.

3. The chances are you will not make it. The crackers are so dry they will stick to your mouth and you won't be able to swallow them without a drink.

In for a Pound

If someone put a £1 coin between two of your fingers, you could easily drop it, couldn't you?

You will need
A £1 coin (or other coin)

1. Put your hands in the position shown in the diagram, with the tips of your ring (third) fingers together and your other fingers folded down so the knuckles are touching.

2. Ask a friend to put the coin between the tips of your ring fingers and hold it there.

3. Now, without sliding your ring fingers apart or moving your knuckles, try to drop the coin. Can you do it? I think you will find that you cannot!

Sweet Victory

Bet a friend they can't pick up a sweet with their teeth and they will happily try to prove you wrong.

But if they do it the way you suggest, you will always win!

You will need
A sweet
A cushion
A friend

1. Ask your friend to kneel down, preferably on a carpet to protect their knees, with the cushion in front of them. Their knees should be together.

2. Ask them to bend over with their forearms on the cushion and their elbows touching their knees, and then put the palms of their hands together.

3. Their hands and forearms should be resting on the cushion. Put the sweet by the tips of their fingers on the cushion.

4. Now ask your friend to straighten up without moving their legs and put their hands behind their back.

5. *Now* ask your friend to pick up the sweet without using their hands. They will almost certainly fall over! (That is why you should always put a cushion in front of them so they don't injure themselves.)

Straw Power

You can drink through a straw, but can you drink through two straws?

You will need
A glass of water
Two drinking straws

1. Put the ends of both straws in your mouth. Then put the other end of one straw in the glass. Let the other end of the second straw dangle in the air.

2. Now try and drink from the straw in the glass. No matter how hard you suck, virtually no water will rise up it because the second straw prevents it from doing so.

Heroic Hoaxes

Game Plan

If you go about playing this game the right way, you will always win.

You will need
20 coins or counters
A friend

1. The aim of the game is to pick up the last coin or counter. At each turn players may pick up one, two or three coins or counters.
2. Spread out the coins or counters on the table and invite your friend to take the first turn. This looks like politeness, but in fact it is crucial to your success.
3. Whatever number of coins or counters your friend picks up, you must pick up a number which makes the total you have both picked up add up to four. So, for example, if your friend picks up one, you pick up three. If he or she picks up two, you pick up two.
4. This way of playing means that the number of coins or counters left on the table can always

be divided by four. By the time your friend has his or her fifth go, there will be just four coins or counters remaining. So whatever number of coins your friend picks up, you can pick up the remainder and thus the last coin. So you will always win providing you let your friend have the first turn.

Unremovable Coin

Bet your friend that they will not be able to remove a coin you stick on their forehead with your magic powers.

You will need
A friend
A small coin such as a penny or 5p piece

1. First demonstrate the trick on yourself. Moisten the coin with spit and stick it on your own forehead. It should stay there until you raise your eyebrows, or frown, when it will fall.
2. Then try the trick on your friend, but instead of sticking the coin to their forehead, just press

a moistened finger firmly on to their skin. Then remove it.

3. Your friend will then try all kinds of contortions to make the coin fall, and will begin to believe you really do have magic powers!

Drenching Drink

Only try this trick on a good friend, outside, on a warm day.

You will need
A friend
A plastic lemonade bottle
A tack or pin
Some water

1. With the tack or pin make a few holes in the bottom of the plastic bottle. Then, holding the bottle over the sink, fill it right to the top with water and screw on its top.

2. Holding the bottle by its top, wipe any water that runs out with a cloth. It will soon stop.

3. Still holding the bottle by its top, offer your friend a drink. He or she will think it is lemonade and will grab it eagerly – only to get soaked! For if you hold the bottle anywhere but by its top, or if you take off the top, the water will pour out of the holes.

Sneaky Trick

Here's a trick to play on a friend that will really exasperate them!

You will need
A mug
A piece of string
A pair of scissors

1. Tie the string round the mug handle and then tie the other end round the door handle, leaving a piece of string hanging loose after tying the knot.

2. Bet your friend that they cannot cut the string without letting the mug fall to the ground and break.

3. When they have spent a few minutes wondering how to do this, you simply cut the piece of string you left hanging loose after tying the knot round the door handle. Very sneaky!

Abracadabra!

Bet someone they cannot make writing appear on a clean piece of paper – then show them how to do it!

You will need
A sheet of paper
Some lemon juice
A lemon squeezer
A small bowl
The cap of a ballpoint pen
A warm radiator

1. The trick is to prepare the paper beforehand. Squeeze some juice from a lemon into a small bowl or eggcup.

invisible

2. Dip the pointed end of the pen cap into the lemon juice and write a message on the paper, as if the juice were ink and the cap a pen.

3. When the juice dries the message will be invisible. Show your friend the paper and bet them you can make a message appear. You can even tell them what it will be!

4. Hold the paper near a warm radiator and, abracadabra, the message will appear!

Inside Out

Bet a friend they can't touch a book outside and inside without opening it.

You will need

A book

1. This is another sneaky trick that may make your friend cross. You have to be careful how you say the original challenge, because, of course, it is all a play on words. Don't, for example, say, 'on the inside and on the outside'.

2. All you do to meet the challenge is to take hold of the book by its cover and touch it with your other hand inside the house, and outside the house! You will then have touched it inside and outside! Of course, you are touching it by holding it, but you can make a point of touching it with the other hand to demonstrate the trick to your friend.

Over the Book

Bet your friend they won't be able to jump over this book if you put it on the floor.

A copy of this book
A friend

1. You need to play this trick indoors. Make the bet, telling your friend the book has magical properties that mean they will not be able to jump over it. Your friend, of course, will not believe you, and will willingly take on the bet.

2. But you will win, because you put the book on the floor *in the corner of the room*! There no one will be able to jump over it!

Shell Power

Bet your friend that he or she cannot break an egg by squeezing it in one hand. It sounds an easy bet to win, doesn't it? Try it and see if it is.

You will need
An egg (uncooked)
A friend

1. You must choose an egg without any cracks or chips in its shell, and your friend must not wear any rings on the hand they use to squeeze the egg.

2. Put the egg into your friend's hand and tell them to squeeze it by putting even pressure on all sides of the shell.

3. Although it sounds like a bet they will win all too easily, the shell of an egg is so strong it is almost impossible to break it by squeezing it in one hand.

Ready-sliced Banana

Bet a friend that you can slice a banana without peeling it.

You will need
A banana
A needle
A friend

1. Offer your friend a banana. Tell them you used magic powers to slice it beforehand.

2. Your friend will peel the banana and be amazed as it falls into slices in their hand!

3. The secret is to prepare the banana a short while before. Stick the needle into the skin at one of the 'seams' and wiggle it so it slices through the fruit. Repeat this at several points all the way along and you will cut the banana into slices.

Don't prepare it too early or the skin will start to go brown where you stuck in the needle and may give the game away.

Not a Drop to Drink

Tease a thirsty friend with this trick.

You will need

A glass of something to drink

A drinking straw

A pin

A friend

1. Prepare the straw by pushing the pin right through it about 2cm from each end.

2. Put the straw in the drink and offer it to your friend. They will not be able to drink through it no matter how hard they try.

3. Take the drink back and cover the two holes at the top of the straw with your fingers as if you are just holding it. You will be able to drink easily, and your friend will be amazed to see the drink passing up the straw!

Rubber Bandjo

Bet a friend they cannot make a musical instrument with a book, some rubber bands and some pencil stubs. Then show them that you can!

You will need
A thin hardback book
Six rubber bands of different lengths and thicknesses
Six pencil stubs or erasers

1. Stretch the rubber bands round the book.
2. Place the pencil stubs or erasers in different positions under the rubber bands.
3. Pluck each rubber band in turn and you will hear a different note.
4. Try moving the pencil stubs or erasers up or down and the note will change. By experimenting with the types of rubber bands and the length of the band that you pluck, you will be able to create a series of notes and, with a bit of practice, play a tune!

Bouncing Hanky

Bet your friend that if you blow your nose on your handkerchief and then throw the handkerchief on the ground it will bounce back to you.

You will need
A cotton handkerchief
A small rubber ball
A rubber band
A friend

1. Prepare the hanky beforehand by wrapping it round the ball and securing the ball in place with the rubber band.

2. When you meet your friend, make the bet with them, then take out your hanky, keeping the ball concealed in your hand.

it will bounce

3. Blow your nose on the hanky, then throw it to the ground. It will bounce back to you! It's a good way of not leaving litter on the ground!

Food Frolic

Only play this trick on a good friend – and make it up to them afterwards!

You will need
To be in a café with a friend

1. When you go into the café order just a drink for yourself, while your friend orders some food.
2. When their food arrives, say, 'I bet you 20p I could eat that sandwich/bun/plate of chips without it touching my mouth.'
3. Your friend will believe your challenge is impossible and will therefore let you try. Whereupon you happily eat their food!
4. Your friend will say, 'Oi, the food is touching your lips! You've lost the bet!'
5. You agree, and hand over the 20p. It's not much to pay for a meal, is it?

In Their Drawers

Bet your friend they cannot put their clothes away in the top drawer of their chest of drawers.

You will need
A chest of drawers
A box
A friend

1. Before you make the bet go to your friend's room and empty everything out of their top drawer. Put the things carefully in the box and hide it in your own room.
2. Take out the drawer, turn it upside down, and replace it in the chest.
3. Make the bet to your friend, and follow them up to their room to prove that you are right.
4. Your friend will be amazed when they open the drawer to put something away and see a solid piece of wood instead of their clothes. You will have won your bet!

Don't forget to give them the box with their clothes in afterwards.

Never Move Again!

Bet a friend you can put them into a position they can never escape from!

You will need
A stool
A paper cup
A broom handle
Some water
A friend

Don't try this trick in a room with a carpet on the floor. If possible, do it in an outhouse or garage.

1. Fill the cup with water, and climb on to the stool holding the cup and the broom handle.
2. Put the cup against the ceiling, and hold it in position with the broom handle. Still holding the broom handle, climb carefully off the stool.

3. Call your friend and ask them if they will hold the broom for you for a moment while you just go and fetch something.

4. Once they are in place, pick up the stool and leave the room. Remind your friend of the bet – they will not dare to move or they will get very wet!

Impossible Drawing I

Bet a friend that they cannot draw the shape shown below without lifting their pen or pencil off the paper.

You will need
A sheet of paper
A pen or pencil
A friend

1. Show your friend the diagram, and make the bet. It will seem impossible.

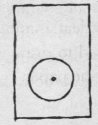

2. When they give up, you can show them how to do it. Fold over the paper and make a dot just below the fold, as shown.

3. Take the pencil up and round in an arc, back to the edge of the paper.

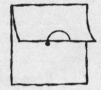

4. Then open up the paper and continue the circle. You have made the drawing without lifting your pencil off the paper!

Impossible Drawing II

Overleaf is another shape you can challenge your friend to draw without taking their pen or pencil off the paper.

You will need

A sheet of paper
A pen or pencil
A friend

1. Your friend will probably try lots of different ways of doing this. But it is unlikely they will succeed.

2. But it is possible. Here's one way of doing it.

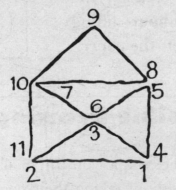

Can you find any other ways?

Five-star Tricks

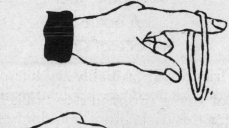

Bottled Apples

I bet you can't get an apple inside a bottle! But if you know how to do it, you just need a little patience.

You will need
An apple tree
A bottle
A piece of string

1. Yes, you do need an apple tree in order to perform this trick, but if you don't have one of your own, you could use one in a friend's garden. Wait until late spring or early summer when the blossom has gone. Where each flower was you will see a tiny fruit forming.

2. Tie the string round the neck of the bottle, leaving about 10cm of loose string on each end, then slip the bottle over one of the little fruits. Push the twig down until the fruit is right inside the bottle, taking care not to damage it, then tie the bottle to the twig.

3. All you have to do now is wait! The fruit will

grow until it is too large to get out of the neck of the bottle, at which point you can cut the twig and remove the string from the bottle.

4. Now bet your friends they can't get an apple into a bottle – and amaze them by proving that you can. Don't tell them how you did it, though!

Cubic Tomatoes

Tomatoes are round, aren't they? I bet you've never seen cube-shaped ones. But, if you know how, you can grow some.

You will need
A tomato plant
Some garden string
Some rubber bands
A small plastic box (measuring
approximately 4cm x 4cm x 4cm)
A paintbrush
Some tomato food
Some potting compost
A 12cm plant pot

1. You can buy tomato plants in spring, or maybe your parents grow them in the garden or greenhouse.

2. When you have bought your plant, pot it in the 12cm pot in compost and water it regularly, once a day or sometimes more often in hot weather. You can keep it on a sunny window sill.

3. When it produces little yellow flowers, gently poke the paintbrush into the centre of each to pollinate it, that is, to transfer some of the yellow pollen from the male part of the flower to the female part so it will produce fruit.

4. After the flowers have shrivelled up, you will see a small, green tomato begin to form behind where each flower was. From now on you will need to feed the plant once a week as well as watering it.

5. Ask an adult to make a hole in the lid of your plastic box large enough for the tomato stem to pass through.

6. Slide the lid on to a stem bearing a fruit, then put the box round the little tomato. Twist a rubber band round the box to hold on the lid,

and tie the box to the stem with garden string. Take great care not to damage the stem or knock the tomato off it, or you will need to start again.

7. All you need to do now is wait until your tomato grows. Keep the plant watered and fed with tomato food.

8. When your tomato has filled the box, pick the fruit, remove the lid, and carefully take the tomato out of the box. If it isn't ripe, put it in a drawer for a few days – and then you can eat it! But not before you've shown it to your friends, having first bet them they've never seen a cubic tomato!

Cubic Eggs

If you can grow a cubic tomato, why not create a cubic egg to go with it?

You will need
A hard-boiled egg
The box from the previous trick, or a similar one
Kitchen paper
Cooking oil
A tin of soup or similar
A refrigerator

1. Boil the egg for about ten minutes, then shell it, taking care not to burn your fingers or damage the egg.
2. Pour a little cooking oil on to some kitchen paper and wipe it all round the inside of the box, to grease it.
3. Gently squash the peeled egg, pointed end downwards, into the box.
4. Put on the lid of the box and stand a tin of soup or something similar on it to weigh it down.

5. When the egg has cooled in the box, put it into the refrigerator for about half an hour. When you take it out, and remove the egg from the box, you will have a cubic egg!

Swimming Paper Fish

Can you make a cut-out paper fish swim in a bath of water without touching it or blowing on it?

You will need
A piece of paper
A pencil
A pair of scissors
Cooking oil
A bath or bowl of water

1. Draw your fish on the paper. At its centre draw a circle, connected by a narrow channel to its tail, as shown in the diagram on the next page. Cut out the fish, the channel and the hole.
2. Fill either a bath or washing-up bowl (depending on the size of the fish) with water

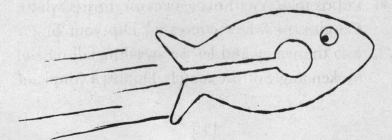

and carefully place the fish on the surface of the water, so its underneath is moistened but its top surface remains dry.

3. Now, how can you make it move without touching it or blowing on it? Challenge your friends to do so. I bet neither you nor they can do it! But it is possible.

4. Here's what you do. Pour one drop of cooking oil into the circular hole in the back of the fish. Oil tries to spread on the surface of water, but the only way it can do this is by travelling down the channel cut into the fish. As it does this it propels the fish forwards – that is, it 'swims' across the surface of the water!

The Moving Match

Can you get a coin into a bottle without touching either it or the bottle?

You will need
An empty bottle
A matchstick
A glass of water
A 5p piece

1. Bend the matchstick so it snaps without breaking completely in two, and place it on the top of the empty bottle. There should be just a few fibres of wood holding the match together.

2. Place the 5p coin on top of the V-shaped match. Now, the challenge is – can you get the coin into the bottle without touching the coin, the match or the bottle?

3. Impossible? Well, no – because this is where the glass of water comes in. Dip your finger into the water and let a few drops fall on the broken angle of the match. Do this a couple of times and you will see the match slowly start to move. The two parts of it move further apart, and as they do so they reach a point where they can no longer support the coin, which, of course, falls into the bottle!

Waterproof Postcard

I bet you can't hold water in an upside-down glass with a postcard! It sounds fantastic – but I can do it!

You will need
A glass tumbler
A picture postcard
Some water

1. Slowly fill the glass with water to the brim, taking care that there are no bubbles in it.
2. Slide the postcard, shiny side down, smoothly across the top of the glass, being careful not to spill the water and also making sure no air gets trapped between the water's surface and the postcard.

3. Press your hand on the postcard and then carefully turn the glass upside down. Just in case it doesn't work first time, do this over the sink or outside in the garden. Take away your hand and – hey presto – the water stays in the glass, held in place by the postcard.

Magic String

Can you make a piece of string rise up in the air – and stay there? I'll bet you can when you've learned how to do it!

You will need
A piece of thin string
A heavy object, such as a mug or book
A metal paper clip
A strong magnet

1. Tie one end of the string to the paper clip, and tie the other end round an object such as a heavy mug, or a hardback book, leaving about 10cm of string between the two.

2. Bring the magnet up to the paper clip. The paper clip will leap on to the magnet.

3. Raise the magnet slowly, so it lifts the paper clip and the string.

4. When the string is stretched straight up in the air, move the magnet a little higher, and the paper clip and string will stand up on end, with no visible means of support! Don't move the magnet too far from the paper clip or the paper clip and string will fall down.

5. To amaze your friends, you could tape the magnet to the underside of a shelf where it cannot be seen, and arrange the string so it is held vertically up in the air permanently.

The Floating Pin

Bet you can't make a pin float on water!

You will need
A glass of water
A pin
A corner of a paper tissue

1. Fill the glass with water, then float the piece of paper tissue on its surface.

2. Carefully put the pin on the tissue.

3. Wait until the tissue becomes saturated with water. When it does so, it will sink to the bottom of the glass, leaving the pin floating on the surface of the water.

it floats!

Unburstable Balloon

Have you ever come across an unburstable balloon. There's no such thing, is there? Well, yes, actually, there is.

You will need
A balloon
A piece of thread
A needle
Some sticky tape
Scissors

1. Blow up the balloon and tie a knot in the neck, or tie the thread round its neck so the air cannot escape.
2. Cut two small pieces of sticky tape and stick them on the balloon in a cross shape.
3. Now try and burst the balloon by sticking the needle through the taped cross. You will find you have created an unburstable balloon!

Strong Paper

Can you stand a glass on a piece of paper which bridges a gap between two other glasses?

You will need
A4 sheet of paper
Three small glasses

1. If you just put the paper across the top of two of the glasses, it would be unwise to try standing the third glass on the top. As you might expect, it would give way, and one or more of the glasses would be likely to get broken.

2. The secret is to fold the paper into a number of pleats, each around 1cm wide, like a concertina. When you have done this, fold your pleated paper in half lengthways.

3. Put two of the glasses about 8cm apart, then place the folded and pleated paper across the top of them, like a bridge. You can now safely stand the third glass on the paper without fear of it breaking.

Heavy Paper

Suppose you were to spread a newspaper out on a table over a stick, do you imagine you could flip it up into the air by hitting the end of the stick? Of course you could, couldn't you? Try it. You'll be surprised!

You will need
A broadsheet newspaper
(e.g. *The Times*, *The Guardian*)
A thin stick 60cm to 100cm long
A table

1. Open up the paper and spread it out on the table with its longer side running along the table's edge.
2. Slide the stick under the centre of the paper, so half of it is under the paper and half of it sticks out over the edge of the table.
3. Smooth out the newspaper so that it is completely flat.
4. Bring your hand down quickly on the stick to flip the paper up into the air.

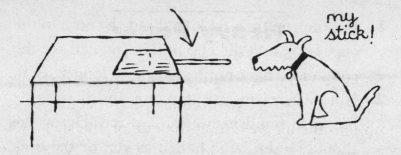

Well, could you do it? It is more likely that you broke the stick. Air pressure holds the paper down on the table, and the only way to lift it up with the stick is to do it slowly, so air gets under the paper. It's a good challenge to try on a friend.

Making Money Appear

We all want to do this, don't we? Here's a clever trick based on a scientific fact which makes a coin magically appear in a seemingly empty cup.

You will need
A cup
A coin
A jug of water
A friend

1. Put the cup on a table and put the coin in the cup. Look into the cup and if you can see the coin, move back until you can no longer see it.
2. Note where you are standing and then get a friend to stand in the same place. He or she should be the same height as you or the trick will not work.
3. Ask your friend if there is a coin in the cup. When they say, 'No', tell them you can make one appear.
4. Pour water slowly from the jug into the cup – and wait for a cry from your friend. The coin will suddenly come into view.

This happens because of a phenomenon called refraction. As light enters water it bends, which makes the image of the coin appear to be higher up than it really is when the cup contains water. This is why, when you look into a pond or a swimming pool, the water appears to be less deep than it really is.

Leaping Paper Clips

Can you make two paper clips leap into the air and link themselves together? This is an amusing trick to show your friends.

You will need

A piece of paper measuring approximately
13cm x 7cm (the size of a £5 note)
Two paper clips

1. Fold the paper into an 'S' shape.
2. Slide one of the paper clips over the front two thicknesses at the top of the paper, with the larger loop of the clip on the side facing you (i.e. the outside of the 'S').
3. Slide the other clip into a similar position on the back two thicknesses, again with the larger loop on the outside.
4. Get hold of one end of the paper in your left hand and the other end in your right and pull them sharply apart. The two paper clips will leap up into the air and link themselves together.

Leaping Rubber Band

Can you make a rubber band leap from one finger to the next? It's very easy when you know how!

You will need
One rubber band about 6cm to 8cm long

1. Hold out your hand – your left hand if you're right-handed and your right hand if you're left-handed – and from the index (first) finger hang the rubber band as shown in the diagram.

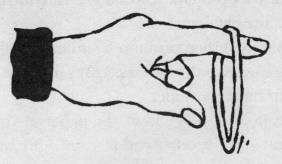

2. Get hold of the end of the rubber band with your other hand, and separate the two strands so one is in front of the other.

3. Wrap the rubber band round your middle finger going under first and then bringing it back over the top. Make sure the two strands stay separated.

4. Slip the free end of the rubber band back over your index finger as shown so it now holds your fingers together.

5. Hold the tied-up index finger with your free hand and bend your middle finger up. The rubber band will leap spectacularly from your index finger to dangle from your middle finger. Clever, isn't it?

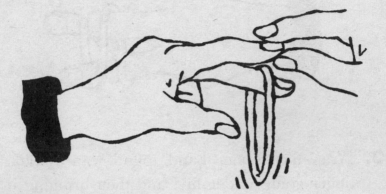

The Practical Joker's Handbook

John Dinneen

Make your friends laugh, scream and blush with this hilarious collection of practical jokes and games ...

Sausage Finger

Take a raw sausage and put it between two of your fingers so that it looks as though you've got five fingers and a thumb on one hand. Now choose a victim and, without letting them see the sausage, shake their hand and say: "Ouch! Mind my bad finger!"
They'll get a nasty shock when you pull your hand away – and leave them holding the sausage!

The Practical Joker's Handbook 2

John Dinneen

More hilarious practical jokes and games to make your friends laugh, scream and blush.

Wet Feet

Ask an adult to help you make small holes in the bottom of a container with a screw top. Now fill the container with water and screw the lid on tightly. The air pressure will stop the water leaking through the holes. Ask a victim to unscrew the lid for you . . . As soon as they do, the water will leak out through the holes and give them a pair of wet feet!